April 26/2009.

To Pastor Dave, from Grateful
hearts — Love eternal in Jesus
Brian & Ronna

QUIET TIMES

with

D.L. MOODY

A Life Essentials Journal

QUIET TIMES
with
D.L. MOODY

COMPILED AND INTRODUCED
BY JAMES S. BELL, JR.

MOODY PRESS
CHICAGO

Library of Congress Cataloging-in-Publication Data

Moody, Dwight Lyman, 1837–1899.
    Quiet times with D.L. Moody / compiled and introduced by James S. Bell, Jr.
        p. cm.
    ISBN ISBN 0-8024-7049-1
    1. Meditations. I. Bell, James S. II. Title
    BV4832.2 .M565 2000
    242--dc21

00-056112

1 3 5 7 9 10 8 6 4 2

Printed in the United States of America

To Brian and Sally Oxley,
whose families have touched many
around the world for Christ

CONTENTS

INTRODUCTION

$\mathscr{E}$ach year hundreds of brand-new Christian books appear not only in Christian bookstores but, increasingly, in secular bookstores and even in retail chain stores throughout the country. It is exciting to see so many topics addressed from a Christian point of view, reaching such a large potential audience with a message of hope and truth.

Though it is important to be relevant and contemporary, this trend may also tend to obscure the fact that there is a huge wealth of Christian classics written over a century ago which are available to help us grow in areas far more important—in the essentials of our relationship with God.

The latest publishing trends may address issues rarely touched upon in the past: taking care of your physical health, raising your teenager, or even the ethics of genetic engineering. But the basics of our relationship with God never change, and it is here, in our response to His love and commandments, where our greatest needs lie, whether they are felt or not.

Our greatest challenges lie in understanding the teachings found in His Word, obeying them, and bearing fruit consistent with the nature and purposes of Christ. It is in these areas that classic Christian works excel. At times we may find that the essentials of the faith get pushed to the periphery in our Christian reading and may be covered superficially even in our devotional life.

One advantage the classics retain in books related to the "Christian living" or "spiritual growth" categories is that they have withstood the scrutiny of succeeding generations. The fruit of the ministries of such great preachers as D.L. Moody, Andrew Murray, and Charles Spurgeon included the conversion of countless thousands of souls as well as strengthening the maturity and impact of the church here and abroad.

The various volumes of Moody, Spurgeon, and Murray have sold millions of copies in numerous editions, and most titles remain on bookstore shelves today. Perhaps one reason for this is that their main target was not the educated elite but the masses. They geared the message of the Gospel to be understood by the average working-class person of the time, and thus their style, by and large, is not archaic today.

I do not mean to imply that they shied away from in-depth biblical knowledge, but rather that they communicated in a simple and straightforward manner as men who truly "knew their Bibles" and had a passion for the average Christian to grow to his or her full stature in Christ.

The preaching and the writings that follow in this Quiet Times series are designed to shake you out of your spiritual lethargy and challenge you to live a life of deeply committed discipleship. They continually focus on the great love of God in Christ and yet specify the need to be like Him and separate from the world. This series is not for complacent Christians who want to merely feel better and enhance the quality of their private lives, but those who want to embark upon the exciting adventure of surrendering all to God. Staying with the essentials, their topics include abiding in Christ, servanthood, prayer, the meaning of the Gospel, the character of God, repentance, and other central teachings and practices at the heart of our walk with God.

Perhaps what makes this series most distinctive is its format. These three great preachers promoted the spiritual disciplines in their ministries, and they wholeheartedly supported biblical meditation and prayer, as well as the application of biblical principles—all of which are found in this journal format.

With the introduction of the LifeEssentials journals that comprise the Quiet Times series, I have attempted to bring together two means of getting closer to God. Most journals today consist of blank pages where we articulate our deepest prayers and monitor our spiritual progress. Yet there is no immediate inspiring text to respond to and record our understanding.

At the same time, solid Christian books of the Moody-Murray-Spurgeon variety allow no room for devotional activity: the opportunity to write prayers, express our understanding of key elements of the text, and make commitments to these same principles. The LifeEssentials journals combine text, prayers, questions, and goals in order to offer the reader a high-quality and satisfying devotional experience.

This book, *Quiet Times with D.L. Moody,* features the writings and words of Dwight Moody, considered by many the greatest evangelist of the nineteenth century. The fifty-two selections can be read daily, occasionally, or weekly. If you choose the latter option, you may wish to record somewhere else how well you achieved your spiritual goals that week.

However you decide to use this journal, it is my profound hope that you will not only have touched the heart of this great preacher and evangelist, but in your quiet moments alone, will have touched the heart of God.

This series is the first release of a forthcoming imprint entitled *LifeEssentials Books*. These books will concentrate on the priorities found at the intersection between faith and living. Based upon what we learn about God and His commands in Scripture, we will be able to better respond in all the critical areas of our lives by being renewed in His image in true holiness.

JAMES S. BELL JR.
Executive Editor
LifeEssentials Books

GOD'S GREAT PATIENCE

$$\boxed{1}$$

Or do you despise the riches of His goodness, forbearance, and longsuffering,
not knowing that the goodness of God leads you to repentance?
ROMANS 2:4

*I*f there is any one thing that I want more than anything else, it is that God may show me everything in my life that is contrary to His will, and that He will give me grace enough to turn from it. I would rather do it—I would rather live so that God should be pleased with me than to have the applause of the world. I would rather live so that God could say, "Well done, good and faithful servant," than just to accumulate a little wealth down here and have the applause of men for a few short years, and then know that I had not pleased Him.

And then how sweet our life will be, how pure our conscience will be, if God has forgiven everything, if we have brought everything to light, and turned from our sins, and the work has been deep and thorough!

But one thought more before I close, and that is, what produces repentance. Paul says in the second chapter of Romans, and the fourth verse: "Or do you despise the riches of His goodness, forbearance, and longsuffering, not knowing that the goodness of God leads you to repentance?"

Oh, that the Lord may open our eyes tonight and show us how good He has been to us all these years.

RESPONDING IN PRAYER

"Lord, shine Your light on every area of sin in my life
and help me to please You alone in everything I do."

Continuing in prayer . . .

_____

_____

_____

_____

_____

_____

_____

When have you been more concerned about pleasing humans rather than God, and what has been the result?

_____

_____

_____

_____

_____

_____

_____

_____

_____

_____

SPIRITUAL GOALS FOR THE WEEK

_____

_____

_____

_____

_____

_____

_____

_____

An Unforgettable Love

2

"Can a mother forget her nursing child, and not have compassion on the son of her womb? . . . Surely they may forget, yet I will not forget you."
ISAIAH 49:15

I love my children more than they love me. They very often say they love me the most. They think they do but it is not true. I used to tell my mother I loved her more than she did me. She would tell it was not so; that she loved me the most. Since I have become a parent I find that is true. God loves us a thousand times more than we can love Him. The apostle says: "In this is love; not that we loved God, but that He loved us" so unlovable, so vile, so polluted. That is a love worth talking about—that God has fixed His love upon us, and that He loves us "with an everlasting love," as we read in Jeremiah.

There is no end to that love; it is everlasting. Your mothers know that there is nothing in your power to do that you will not do for your children, that is for their good. There are some things you will withhold from them because you love them too much to grant all their wishes; and they think you don't love them because you do not grant their wishes. So, sometimes, we think God doesn't love us because He doesn't grant all our requests and doesn't answer all our prayers just in the time and place that we would have them answered. A mother's love may be very strong, but it is not to be compared with the love of God.

RESPONDING IN PRAYER

"Lord, just because I don't always get the exact answers to prayer that I desire, help me to remember that Your love and care for me are still perfect."

Continuing in prayer . . .

In what ways has God "remembered" you by showing mercy and compassion in
difficult times?

_____

_____

_____

_____

_____

_____

_____

_____

_____

SPIRITUAL GOALS FOR THE WEEK

_____

_____

_____

_____

_____

_____

_____

_____

RESURRECTED FROM OUR SINS

3

For all have sinned and fall short of the glory of God, being justified
freely by His grace through the redemption that is in Christ Jesus.
ROMANS 3:23–24

When Christ met that poor widow coming out of Nain, following the body of her darling boy to the grave—he was just newly dead—His loving heart could not pass her; He stopped the funeral and bade the dead arise. He was obeyed at once, and the mother was clasped once more in the living embrace of her son. And when Jesus stood by the grave of Lazarus, who had been dead four days, was it not just as easy for Him to say, "Lazarus, come forth!"? Was it not as easy for Him to bring Lazarus from his tomb, who had been dead four days, as the son of the widow, who had been dead but one? Yes, it was just as easy; there was no difference. They were both alike dead, and Christ raised the one just as easily, and as willingly, and as lovingly as the other.

And therefore, my friend, you need not complain that Christ cannot save you. Christ died for the ungodly, and if you turn to Him at this moment with an honest heart, and receive Him simply as your Savior and your God, I have the authority of His Word (John 6:37) for telling you that He will by no means cast you out.

And you who have never felt the burden of your sin—you who think there is a great deal of difference—you who thank God that you are not as other men—beware! God has nothing to say to the self-righteous. Unless you humble yourself before Him in the dust, and confess before Him your iniquities and sins, the gate of heaven, which is open only for sinners saved by grace, must be shut against you forever!

RESPONDING IN PRAYER

"Lord, just as You have given me new life at conversion,
raise me up from the deadness of recent sin that
I may experience deeper fellowship with You."

Continuing in prayer . . .

How has humility before God brought you closer to Him?

_____

_____

_____

_____

_____

_____

_____

_____

_____

SPIRITUAL GOALS FOR THE WEEK

_____

_____

_____

_____

_____

_____

_____

_____

_____

_____

THE NATURE OF FAITH

---- 4 ----

Now faith is the substance of things hoped for,
the evidence of things not seen.
HEBREWS 11:1

Faith is not some mysterious feeling that we discover within ourselves, but simply the natural results of knowing Christ, both through the Scriptures, and in our lives. Faith is an outward look and not an inward view.

Many people complain that they are unable to believe what they cannot see, and do not realize that, even in making the statement, they contradict themselves. Faith that requires proof isn't faith at all. To believe a person, or a truth, implies that by experience we do not know it or cannot understand it, but accept it on the statement of another.

I am not a chemist, and I do not know anything about the results of certain drugs upon my body. Yet if I should be advised to take a certain medicine, I would have to depend fully upon the wisdom of the man from whom I bought it. I would have to exercise faith in him. If, however, I had been trained in the business, and could assure myself of the purity of every ingredient of the prescription, I would then have no need to exercise my faith, for I would then know and see. Faith is simply believing in God and acting upon one's trust in Him, appropriating His blessings individually.

RESPONDING IN PRAYER

"Lord, grant me the ability to believe in You whom I cannot see
and trust You to bless me according to Your Word."

Continuing in prayer . . .

_____

_____

_____

_____

_____

_____

_____

How can you better act upon the trust you have in God and take hold of the promises He makes in Scripture?

_____

_____

_____

_____

_____

_____

_____

_____

_____

_____

SPIRITUAL GOALS FOR THE WEEK

_____

_____

_____

_____

_____

_____

_____

_____

_____

KNOWING GOD

| 5 |

*But as many as received Him, to them He gave the right
to become children of God, even to those who believe in His name.*
JOHN 1:12

*B*eware of ignorance and indifference. You cannot afford to neglect your soul. There is too much at stake. I never knew an idle man to be converted. Until he wakes up and realizes his lost and hopeless condition, God Almighty will not reach down and take him by the hand. A ship was once in great danger at sea, and all but one man were on their knees. They called to him to come and join them in prayer, but he replied:

"Not I; it's your business to look after the ship. I'm only a passenger."

Remember that mere knowledge is not enough. Many a man knows the Gospel precepts and promises by heart who is not touched by saving grace. Knowledge is often useless or positively harmful, and what we want is to know God's will and observe it. Even good resolutions are not enough. No doubt they are helpful in their way, but the Bible does not lead us to believe that they can save a man. It does not say: "As many as *resolved to receive* Him, to them gave He power to become the sons of God, even to them that *resolve to believe* on His name"; it says: "But as many as received Him . . . to those who believe in His name."

RESPONDING IN PRAYER

*"Lord, I want to know about You from Your Word, but more importantly,
I want to know You intimately and personally by Your Spirit."*

Continuing in prayer . . .

_____

_____

_____

_____

_____

_____

FOR REFLECTION

What truths in the Word would you like to experience in a more personal way in your daily living?

_____

_____

_____

_____

_____

_____

_____

_____

_____

_____

_____

SPIRITUAL GOALS FOR THE WEEK

_____

_____

_____

_____

_____

_____

_____

_____

FINISHING THE WORK

6

"For I, the Lord your God, will hold your right hand,
saying to you, 'Fear not, I will help you.'"
ISAIAH 41:13

*N*ow if God has got hold of my right hand in His, cannot He hold me and keep me? Has not God the power to keep? The great God who made heaven and earth can keep a poor sinner like you and like me, if we trust Him. To refrain from feeling confidence in God for fear of falling would be like a man who refused a pardon, for fear that he should get into prison again; or a drowning man who refused to be rescued, for fear of falling into the water again.

Many men look forth at the Christian life and fear that they will not have sufficient strength to hold out to the end. They forget the promise that "as your days, so shall your strength be" (Deuteronomy 33:25). It reminds me of the clock pendulum, which grew disheartened at the thought of having to travel so many thousands of miles; but when it reflected that the distance was to be accomplished by "tick, tick, tick," it took fresh courage to go its daily journey.

So it is the special privilege of the Christian to commit himself to the keeping of his heavenly Father and to trust Him day by day. It is a great comforting thing to know that the Lord will not begin the good work without finishing it.

RESPONDING IN PRAYER

"Lord, I will not fear falling away from You because
You have the power to keep me until Your work in me is finished."

Continuing in prayer . . .

Make a commitment for fresh courage to follow God on your daily journey and have a deep sense of His ability to keep you faithful.

_____

_____

_____

_____

_____

_____

_____

_____

_____

SPIRITUAL GOALS FOR THE WEEK

_____

_____

_____

_____

_____

_____

_____

_____

_____

HOPE THAT IS CERTAIN

7

"I know that my Redeemer lives, and He shall stand at last on the earth."
JOB 19:25

*D*o you think that the God who has justified me will condemn me? That is quite an absurdity. God is going to save us so that neither men, angels, nor devils can bring any charge against us or Him. He will have the work complete.

Job lived in a darker day than we do; but we read in Job 19:25: "I know that my Redeemer lives, and He shall stand at last on the earth."

The same confidence breathes through Paul's last words to Timothy: "For this reason I also suffer these things; nevertheless I am not ashamed, for I know whom I have believed and am persuaded that He is able to keep what I have committed to Him until that Day." It is not a matter of doubt, but of knowledge. "I know." "I am *convinced*." The word *hope* is not used in the Scriptures to express doubt. It is used in regard to the second coming of Christ, or to the resurrection of the body. We do not say that we "hope" we are Christians. I do not say that I "hope" I am an American or that I "hope" I am a married man. These are settled things.

And so, if we are born of God we know it; and He will not leave us in darkness if we search the Scriptures.

RESPONDING IN PRAYER

"Lord, please make my hope in Your deliverance an absolute certainty, knowing that You can completely save me through to the last day."

Continuing in prayer . . .

What are you entrusting to God with the firm hope that He will accomplish it
(according to His purposes) when your life is finished?

_____

_____

_____

_____

_____

_____

_____

_____

_____

_____

SPIRITUAL GOALS FOR THE WEEK

_____

_____

_____

_____

_____

_____

_____

_____

A SURE FOUNDATION

───┤ 8 ├───

In God I have put my trust; I will not fear. What can flesh do to me?
PSALM 56:4

It is better to trust in the Lord than to put confidence in man" (Psalm 118:8). You will say "Amen" to that. You that have put confidence in man and have been disappointed can say that is true. Every infidel will admit that. It is better to trust God than yourself. I would rather trust God than my own deceitful heart. It is better to make yourself a liar and make God true. It is better to trust in the Lord than to put confidence even in princes. That is what the Lord said.

The psalmist says, "In God I have put my trust; I will not fear. What can flesh do to me?" Why? Because his heart is fixed—trusting.

If God has hid me in the secret pavilion, let men slander me and abuse me if they like! If I can say that God is my Father, Jesus is my Savior, and heaven is my home; let the world rail—let the flesh do what it pleases—I will not be afraid of evil tidings, for my trust is in God! Is not that a good footing for eternity? "Heaven and earth will pass away, but My words will by no means pass away." If you get your feet fair and square on the rock, let the waves beat if they will. A Christian once said that he trembled sometimes, but the foundation never did: He had his foot upon the rock. We want good footing for eternity, and there is not better footing than the Word of God.

RESPONDING IN PRAYER

"Lord, don't let my foot slip, but keep me secure on the solid foundation of Jesus Christ, rather than the strength which the world offers."

Continuing in prayer . . .

_____

_____

_____

_____

_____

_____

What are some of the earthly foundations that you have tried and that have failed in your life?

_____

_____

_____

_____

_____

_____

_____

_____

_____

_____

SPIRITUAL GOALS FOR THE WEEK

_____

_____

_____

_____

_____

_____

_____

_____

_____

_____

GRACE TRIUMPHANT

9

*Jesus answered and said to her, "If you knew the gift of God,
and who it is who says to you, 'Give Me a drink,' you would
have asked Him, and He would have given you living water."*

JOHN 4:10

*S*ee how the grace of God could save a Mary Magdalene possessed of seven devils! Ask her what it was that melted her heart, and she would tell you that it was the grace of God. Look again at that woman whom Christ met at the well at Sychar. The Savior offered her a cup of the living water. She drank, and now she walks the crystal pavement of heaven. See how the grace of God could change Zacchaeus, the hated publican of Jericho! Now he is in yonder world of light; he was brought there by the sovereign grace of God.

You will have noticed that many of those who were about the most unlikely have, by the power of God's grace, become very eminent in His service. Look at the twelve apostles of Christ; they were all unlettered men. This ought to encourage all whose education is limited to give themselves to God's work. When our earthly work is ended, then, like our Master, we shall enter into glory.

It has been well remarked, "Grace is glory militant; and glory is grace triumphant. Grace is glory begun; glory is grace made perfect. Grace is the first degree of glory; glory is the highest degree of grace."

RESPONDING IN PRAYER

*"Lord, I thank You for Your grace,
which can transform even the most hardened sinner."*

Continuing in prayer . . .

FOR REFLECTION

What has it meant in your life to drink deeply of the living water of Christ?

_____

_____

_____

_____

_____

_____

_____

_____

_____

_____

SPIRITUAL GOALS FOR THE WEEK

_____

_____

_____

_____

_____

_____

_____

_____

_____

_____

OVERLOOKING FAULTS

10

Love suffers long and is kind; love does not envy; love does not parade itself,
is not puffed up; does not behave rudely, does not seek its own, is not
provoked, thinks no evil; does not delight in iniquity, but rejoices in the truth.

1 CORINTHIANS 13:4–6

*L*ove will rebuke evil, but will not rejoice in it. Love will be impatient of sin, but patient with the sinner. To form the habit of finding fault constantly is very damaging to spiritual life; it is about the lowest and meanest position that a man can take. I never saw a man who was aiming to do the best work, but there could have been some improvement. I never did anything in my life, I never addressed an audience, that I didn't think I could have done it better; but to sit down and find fault with other people when we are doing nothing ourselves, not lifting our hands to save someone, is all wrong, and is the opposite of holy, patient, divine love.

Love is forbearance; and what we want is to get this spirit of criticism and faultfinding out of the church and out of our hearts; and let each one of us live as if we had to answer for ourselves and not for the community at the last day. If we are living according to the thirteenth chapter of 1 Corinthians, we will not be all the time finding fault with other people. "Love suffers long and is kind." Love forgets itself and doesn't dwell upon itself.

RESPONDING IN PRAYER

"Lord, help me to take a firm stand against sin but not always be
trying to find it in others; rather let me realize that I too have faults."

Continuing in prayer . . .

_____

_____

_____

_____

_____

_____

When has your own faultfinding been a form of self-righteousness or judgmen-
talism, when you could have put more time into patient love?

_____

_____

_____

_____

_____

_____

_____

_____

_____

_____

_____

_____

_____

SPIRITUAL GOALS FOR THE WEEK

_____

_____

_____

_____

_____

_____

_____

_____

_____

A JOYFUL CHURCH

11

"The joy of the Lord is your strength."
NEHEMIAH 8:10

*O*h! The reward that is in store for those who serve Him! We have this joy, if we serve Him. A man or woman is not fit to work for God who is cast down, because they go about their work with a telltale face. "The joy of the Lord is your strength."

What we need today is a joyful church. A joyful church will make inroads upon the works of Satan, and we will see the Gospel going down into dark lanes and dark alleys, and into dark garrets and cellars, and we will see the drunkards reached and the gamblers and the harlots come pressing into the kingdom of God. It is this carrying a sad countenance, with so many wrinkles on our brows, that retards Christianity. Oh, may there come great joy upon believers everywhere, that we may shout for joy and rejoice in God day and night.

A joyful church—let us pray for that, that the Lord may make us joyful. When we have joy, then we will have success; and if we don't have the reward we think we should have here, let us constantly remember the rewarding time will come hereafter.

RESPONDING IN PRAYER

*"Lord, may I realize that true joy is the key
to success in our calling, leading to eternal rewards."*

Continuing in prayer . . .

Reflect on how the element of joy in your life might help accomplish the goals of your witness for Christ.

_____

_____

_____

_____

_____

_____

_____

_____

_____

SPIRITUAL GOALS FOR THE WEEK

_____

_____

_____

_____

_____

_____

_____

_____

_____

_____

DARE TO DO RIGHT

─── 12 ───

Enoch walked with God; and he was not, for God took him.
GENESIS 5:24

A great deal is being said about holiness. Every true child of God desires to be holy, as his Father in heaven is holy. And holiness is walking with God. Enoch had only one object. How simple life becomes when we have only one object to seek, one purpose to fulfill—to walk with God—to please God! It has been said that the utmost many Christians get to is that they are pardoned criminals. How short they fall of the joy and blessedness of walking with God!

I will venture to say that Enoch, in his day, was considered a most singular and visionary man—an "eccentric" man—the most peculiar man who lived in that day. He was a man out of fashion—out of the fashion of this world, which passes away. He would not have gone with the multitude to do evil. He would have taken that high ground, though the whole world were against him. And what we want is the moral courage to be against the whole world when we are in the right. Enoch dared to do right. He took his position, and dared to stand against an ungodly generation.

RESPONDING IN PRAYER

*"Lord, help me take the risk of being out of fashion with
this world by walking in full obedience to Your commands."*

Continuing in prayer . . .

_____

_____

_____

_____

_____

_____

_____

_____

_____

What does it mean in your life to stand against the crowd because you walk with God in an uncompromising manner?

_____

_____

_____

_____

_____

_____

_____

_____

_____

SPIRITUAL GOALS FOR THE WEEK

_____

_____

_____

_____

_____

_____

_____

_____

A LIGHT BURDEN

13

"Come to Me, all you who labor and are heavy laden,
and I will give you rest. Take My yoke upon you and learn from Me,
for I am gentle and lowly in heart, and you will find rest for your souls.
For My yoke is easy and My burden is light."

MATTHEW 11:28–30

To Peter and James and John, on the mount of transfiguration, He says again, "This is My beloved Son. Hear Him!" And that voice went echoing and reechoing through Palestine, through all the earth from sea to sea; yes, that voice is echoing still, *"Hear Him! Hear Him!"*

My friend, will you hear Him now? Hark! What is He saying to you? "Come to Me, all you who labor and are heavy laden, and I will give you rest. Take My yoke upon you and learn from Me, for I am gentle and lowly in heart, and you will find rest for your souls. For My yoke is easy and My burden is light." Will you not think well of such a Savior? Will you not believe in Him? Will you not trust in Him with all your heart and mind? Will you not live for Him? If He laid down His life for us, is it not the least we can do to lay down ours for Him? If He bore the cross and died on it for me, ought I not be willing to take it up for Him? Oh, have we not reason to think well of Him? Do you think it is right and noble to lift up your voice against such a Savior? Do you think it is just to cry "Crucify Him! Crucify Him!"?

Oh, may God help all of us to glorify the Father by thinking well of His only begotten Son.

RESPONDING IN PRAYER

"Lord, when I think of what You have done for me on the cross,
I realize that I can handle everything in life through You."

Continuing in prayer . . .

Pray for a greater ability to spiritually hear God as He speaks through your circumstances and through other people.

_____

_____

_____

_____

_____

_____

_____

_____

_____

_____

SPIRITUAL GOALS FOR THE WEEK

_____

_____

_____

_____

_____

_____

_____

_____

BELIEF IN THE UNSEEN

14

"Blessed are those who have not seen and yet have believed."
JOHN 20:29

We do not find that the Gospel story was exaggerated by generation after generation. It did not grow as the years passed away. It was put in writing within twenty-five years after the event happened. There was no disagreement regarding it among the early disciples until Greek converts at Corinth imported Greek sentiment regarding the Resurrection into their creed, only to draw from Paul the invincible logic of the epistle to the Corinthians.

We are sometimes inclined to envy those early disciples. We think that if we saw Him and touched Him and heard Him speak peace to our souls, all our doubts and questionings would disappear forever. Our blessed Master foresaw our difficulties, and looking down the centuries He said to doubting Thomas, "Because you have seen Me, you have believed. Blessed are those who have not seen and yet have believed."

Arguments may not satisfy your mind, but the Spirit of God can bear witness in your heart. "Blessed are those who have not seen and yet have believed." Oh, may God help us to realize the precious truth that we are not worshiping a dead Savior! He is risen from the dead and has ascended into heaven, and in such a day and hour as we know not He will return. God help us to be faithful until He calls us.

RESPONDING IN PRAYER

"Lord, the unseen world of Your kingdom sometimes seems unreal to me; help me to realize that You reign in my life from the heavenly places."

Continuing in prayer . . .

_____

_____

_____

_____

_____

_____

How can you be more faithful to Christ by living within the reality of His unseen lordship over all things?

_____

_____

_____

_____

_____

_____

_____

_____

_____

_____

SPIRITUAL GOALS FOR THE WEEK

_____

_____

_____

_____

_____

_____

_____

_____

ZEALOUS SERVANTS

---15---

But Jesus answered them, "My Father has been working
until now, and I have been working."

JOHN 5:17

"Zeal without knowledge!" I think I have heard that objection ever since I commenced the Christian life. I heard of someone who was speaking the other day of something that was to be done, and who said he hoped zeal would be tempered with moderation. Another friend very wisely replied that he hoped moderation would be tempered with zeal. If that were always the case, Christianity would be like a red-hot ball rolling over the face of the earth. There is no power on earth that can stand before the onward march of God's people when they are in dead earnest.

In all ages, God has used those who were in earnest. Satan always calls idle men into his service. God calls active and earnest—not indolent—men and women. When we are thoroughly aroused and ready for His work, then He will take us up and use us. You remember where Elijah found Elisha; he was plowing in the field—he was at work. Gideon was at the threshing floor. Moses was away in Horeb looking after the sheep. None of these eminent servants of God were indolent men; what they did, they did with all their might.

We want such men and women nowadays. If we cannot do God's work with all the knowledge we would like, let us at any rate do it with all the zeal that God has given us.

RESPONDING IN PRAYER

"Lord, help me get rid of my excuses for not serving You
with all my might and work to the best of my ability
with the gifts You have given me."

Continuing in prayer . . .

_____

_____

_____

_____

_____

What are your greatest fears, reservations, excuses, etc., for not serving God with everything He's given you?

_____

_____

_____

_____

_____

_____

_____

_____

_____

_____

SPIRITUAL GOALS FOR THE WEEK

_____

_____

_____

_____

_____

_____

_____

_____

CRITICAL QUESTIONS

| 16 |

For the word of God is living and powerful, and sharper than any two-edged
sword, piercing even to the division of soul and spirit, and of joints and
marrow, and is a discerner of the thoughts and intents of the heart.

HEBREWS 4:12

It would be a good thing if questions like these were pasted in the front of
every Bible:

1. What persons have I read about, and what have I learned about them?
2. What places have I read about, and what have I read about them? If the place is
   not mentioned, can I find out where it is? Do I know its position on the map?
3. Does the passage refer to any particular time in the history of the children of
   Israel or of some leading character?
4. Can I tell from memory what I have just been reading?
5. Are there any parallel passages or tests that throw light on this passage?
6. Have I read anything about God the Father? Or about Jesus Christ? Or about
   the Holy Spirit?
7. What have I read about myself? About man's sinful nature? About the spiritual
   new nature?
8. Is there any duty for me to observe? Any example to follow? Any promise to
   lay hold of? Any exhortation for my guidance? Any prayer that I may echo?
9. How is this Scripture profitable for doctrine? for reproof? for correction? for
   instruction in righteousness?
10. Does it contain the Gospel in type or in evidence?
11. What is the key verse of the chapter or passage? Can I repeat it from memory?

RESPONDING IN PRAYER

"Lord, help me to take these questions seriously as I study Your Word,
and please speak to me as I try to answer them."

Continuing in prayer . . .

_____

_____

_____

_____

FOR REFLECTION

Choose three questions from the list and apply them to your next reading of Scripture. Put your findings in the lines that follow.

_____

_____

_____

_____

_____

_____

_____

_____

_____

_____

_____

_____

SPIRITUAL GOALS FOR THE WEEK

_____

_____

_____

_____

_____

_____

_____

_____

_____

_____

_____

_____

INFLUENCE VERSUS POWER

─────┤ 17 ├─────

On the last day, that great day of the feast, Jesus stood and cried out, saying, "If anyone thirsts, let him come to Me and drink. He who believes in Me, as the Scripture has said, out of his heart will flow rivers of living water."
JOHN 7:37–38

There is a difference between influence and power. The high priests and the Pharisees had influence; Peter and the apostles after Pentecost had power.

There is a difference between the indwelling of the Holy Ghost and His filling one with power. Every true child of God, who has been cleansed by the blood of Christ, is a temple or dwelling place of the Holy Ghost. But yet he may not have fullness of power.

In the third chapter of John, Nicodemus went to Jesus by night to get light, and I have no doubt he got it; but he did not receive it in abundance, or he wouldn't have stayed in the Sanhedrin three years, listening to all the mean, cutting things they said of Jesus. It took the death of Christ to bring him out manfully and boldly.

Four walls cannot contain the influence of a man who is full of the Holy Ghost and power. "Rivers of living water"! Think of the rivers that flowed from Charles H. Spurgeon and George Mueller! Let us pray for this power. The disciples were told to wait because the Spirit was not yet given, but we do not have to wait now, because the Holy Spirit is here. The power of the Holy Ghost is one thing that can save the church and save our country.

RESPONDING IN PRAYER

"Lord, at times I define success and achievement by the influence I bring to bear on people and situations. But what I really desire is Your power in my life, regardless of the recognition I receive."

Continuing in prayer . . .

_____

_____

_____

_____

_____

When have you in the past confused influence with power? How in the long run does spiritual power produce even greater influence, though it may not be as recognized?

_____

_____

_____

_____

_____

_____

_____

_____

_____

_____

SPIRITUAL GOALS FOR THE WEEK

_____

_____

_____

_____

_____

_____

_____

A CLEAN SOUL

─────┤18├─────

Then He put out His hand and touched him, saying, "I am willing;
be cleansed." Immediately the leprosy left him.

LUKE 5:13

*H*e will speak to you as He did to that poor leper and say, "I am willing; be cleansed," and the leprosy of your sins will flee away from you. It is the Lord, and the Lord alone, who can forgive sins. If you say to Him, "Lord, I have a terrible temper; You can make me clean"; "Lord, I have a deceitful heart. Cleanse me, O Lord; give me a new heart. O Lord, give me the power to overcome the flesh and the snares of the devil!" "Lord, I am full of unclean habits." If you come to Him with a sincere spirit, you will hear the voice, "I am willing; be cleansed." It will be done. Do you think that the God who created the world out of nothing, who by a breath put life into the world—do you think that if He says, "Thou shalt be cleansed," you will not?

Now, you can make a wonderful exchange today. You can have health in the place of sickness; you can get rid of everything that is vile and hateful in the sight of God. The Son of God comes down and says, "I will take away your leprosy and give you health in its stead. I will take away that terrible disease that is ruining your body and soul and give you My righteousness in its stead. I will clothe you with the garments of salvation."

RESPONDING IN PRAYER

"Lord, it is so encouraging to know that You can cleanse me
of any and all sin and give me a new heart like Yours."

Continuing in prayer . . .

_____

_____

_____

_____

_____

_____

Ask God to clothe you with the garments of salvation and reveal any area of your life that remains unclean. What areas need His cleansing touch?

_____

_____

_____

_____

_____

_____

_____

_____

_____

_____

SPIRITUAL GOALS FOR THE WEEK

_____

_____

_____

_____

_____

_____

_____

_____

EVERYDAY CHRISTIANITY

19

The Lord knows how to deliver the godly out of temptations and to reserve
the unjust under punishment for the day of judgment.

2 PETER 2:9

If I wanted to find out whether a man was a Christian, I wouldn't go to his minister. I would go and ask his wife. I tell you, we want more home piety just now. If a man doesn't treat his wife right, I don't want to hear him talk about Christianity. What is the use of his talking about salvation for the next life if he has no salvation for this? We want a Christianity that goes into our homes and everyday lives.

Some men's religion just repels me. They put on a whining voice and a sort of a religious tone and talk so sanctimoniously on Sunday that you would think they were wonderful saints. But on Monday they are quite different. They put their religion away with their clothes, and you don't see any more of it until the next Sunday. You laugh, but let us look out that we don't belong to that class.

My friends, we have got to have a higher type of Christianity, or the church is gone. It is wrong for men and women to profess what they don't possess. If you are not overcoming temptations, the world is overcoming you. Just get on your knees and ask God to help you. My friends, let us go to God and ask Him to search us. Let us ask Him to wake us up, and let us not think that just because we are church members we are all right. We are all wrong if we are not getting victory over sin.

RESPONDING IN PRAYER

"Lord, help me to take the religion I express on Sunday
and bring it into my home and workplace on Monday."

Continuing in prayer . . .

_____

_____

_____

_____

_____

FOR REFLECTION

Examine what you profess but may not yet possess. Ask God to show you how to live what you believe and forsake sin in the critical areas of your life.

SPIRITUAL GOALS FOR THE WEEK

GLORIOUS GOOD NEWS

── 20 ──

Rejoice in the Lord always. Again I will say, rejoice!
PHILIPPIANS 4:4

*W*ith nine "blesseds" or "happys," Christ began his Sermon on the Mount: Blessed are the poor in spirit; blessed are those who mourn; blessed are the meek; blessed are those who hunger and thirst for righteousness. Jesus continued, "Blessed are the pure in heart, . . . blessed are the peacemakers, . . . blessed are those who are persecuted for righteousness' sake, . . . blessed are you when they revile and persecute you, and say all kinds of evil against you falsely for My sake" (see Matthew 5:3–11). Blessed, blessed, blessed! Happy, happy, happy!

Glorious good news for the young as through Christ they may have their coming years ennobled, and for a lifetime all the angels of God their coadjutants and all the armies of heaven their allies! Glorious good news for the middle-aged as through Christ they may have their perplexities disentangled, and their courage rallied, and their victory over all obstacles and hindrances made forever sure! Glorious good news for the aged as they may have the sympathy of Him of whom St. John wrote: "His head and hair were white like wool, as white as snow," and the defense of the everlasting arms! Glorious good news for the dying as they may have ministering spirits to escort them, and opening gates to receive them, and a sweep of eternal glories to encircle them, and the welcome of a loving God to embosom them!

RESPONDING IN PRAYER

*"Lord, I am indeed gloriously blessed in all the stages of my life
and through all eternity because of what You have done for me."*

Continuing in prayer . . .

_____

_____

_____

_____

_____

_____

What is the glorious news for you at your stage and condition in life, and how might you better thank God for it?

_____

_____

_____

_____

_____

_____

_____

_____

_____

SPIRITUAL GOALS FOR THE WEEK

_____

_____

_____

_____

_____

_____

_____

WHAT MONEY CAN'T BUY

─────┤21├─────

"Sell what you have and give alms; provide yourselves money bags
which do not grow old, a treasure in the heavens that does not fail,
where no thief approaches nor moth destroys.
For where your treasure is, there your heart will be also."

LUKE 12:33–34

*I*t is a great mistake to make so much of riches as we do. But there are some riches that we cannot praise too much, that never pass away. They are the treasures laid up in heaven for those who truly belong to God.

No matter how rich or elevated we may be here, there is always something that we want. The greatest chance the rich have over the poor is the one they enjoy the least—that of making themselves happy. Worldly riches never make anyone truly happy. We all know, too, that they often take wings and fly away. It is said of Midas that whatever he touched turned into gold, but with his long ears he was not much the better for it.

There is a great deal of truth in some of these old fables. Money, like time, ought not to be wasted, but I pity that man who has more of either than he knows how to use. There is no truer saying than that man, by doing good with his money, makes it pass as currency for the merchandise of heaven; but all the wealth of the universe would not buy a man's way there. Salvation must be taken as a gift for the asking. There is no man so poor in this world that he may not be a heavenly millionaire.

RESPONDING IN PRAYER

"Lord, I want to make the best use of my money for Your kingdom
so that I can make the most of earthly wealth."

Continuing in prayer . . .

_____

_____

_____

_____

_____

Where do you store up your treasures, and what does your heart seek for true happiness?

_____

_____

_____

_____

_____

_____

_____

_____

_____

_____

SPIRITUAL GOALS FOR THE WEEK

_____

_____

_____

_____

_____

_____

_____

_____

_____

THE LIGHT OF HEAVEN

|22|

*There shall be no night there: They need no lamp nor light of the sun,
for the Lord God gives them light. And they shall reign forever and ever.*
REVELATION 22:5

*A*ll the joys we are to know in heaven will come from the presence of God.
This is the leading thought in all that the Scripture has to say on the subject.
What life on this earth is without health, life in heaven would be without the
presence of God. God's presence will be the very light and life of the place. It is
said that one translation of the world describing the presence of God is "a happy-
making sight." It will be a sight like the return of a long-lost boy to his mother,
or the first glimpse of your home after you have been a long time away.

Some of you know how a little sunshine on a dark day, or the face of a kind
friend in trouble, often cheers us up. Well, it will be something like that, only a
thousand times better. Our perceptions of God will be clearer then, and that will
make us love Him all the more.

The more we know God, the more we love Him. A great many of us would
love God more if we only became better acquainted with Him. While on earth, it
gives Christians great pleasure to think of the perfection of Jesus Christ, but how
will it be when we see Him as He is?

RESPONDING IN PRAYER

*"Lord, grant me a greater experience of Your presence in my life
so that I may have a foretaste of heaven
and trust You to bless me according to Your Word."*

Continuing in prayer . . .

_____

_____

_____

_____

_____

_____

What can you do today related to your spiritual activities that will allow you to see Christ more clearly and love Him even more?

_____

_____

_____

_____

_____

_____

_____

_____

SPIRITUAL GOALS FOR THE WEEK

_____

_____

_____

_____

_____

_____

_____

_____

PRAYER BASED ON SCRIPTURE

But may the God of all grace, who called us to His eternal glory
by Christ Jesus, after you have suffered a while,
perfect, establish, strengthen, and settle you.
1 PETER 5:10

In the gospel of John we read: "If you (that "if" is a mountain to begin with), "If you abide in Me, and My words abide in you, you will ask what you desire, and it shall be done for you" (15:7). The latter part is often quoted, but not the first. Why, there is very little abiding in Christ nowadays! You go and visit Him once in a while; but that is all. If Christ is in my heart, of course I will not ask anything that is against His will. And how many of us have God's Word abiding in us?

We must have a warrant for our prayers. If we have some great desire, we must search the Scriptures to find if it be right to ask for it. There are many things we want that are not good for us; and many other things we desire to avoid that are really our best blessings. A friend of mine was shaving one morning, and his little boy, not four years old, asked him for his razor, and said he wanted to whittle with it. When he found he could not get it, he began to cry as if his heart would break. I am afraid that there are a great many of us who are praying for razors. John Bunyan blessed God for that Bedford jail more than for anything else that happened to him in this life. We never pray for affliction; and yet it is often the best thing we could ask.

RESPONDING IN PRAYER

"Lord, please let me realize that afflictions that come my way
can be great blessings because they draw me closer to You,
allowing me to be more like You."

Continuing in prayer . . .

Ask God to reveal those things that you may want but may really not be good for you, as well as those things which you might try to avoid but may be good for you. Then list below those not-so-good wants as well as those good-but-not-always-wanted things.

_____

_____

_____

_____

_____

_____

_____

_____

_____

_____

SPIRITUAL GOALS FOR THE WEEK

_____

_____

_____

_____

_____

_____

_____

_____

_____

ANSWERS TO PRAYER

|24|

"Ask, and it will be given to you; seek, and you will find; knock, and it will be opened to you. For everyone who asks receives, and he who seeks finds, and to him who knocks it will be opened."

MATTHEW 7:7–8

*T*oo often we knock at mercy's door, and then run away, instead of waiting for an entrance and an answer. Thus we act as if we were afraid of having our prayers answered.

A great many people pray in that way; they do not wait for the answer. Our Lord teaches us here that we are not only to ask, but we are to wait for the answer; if it does not come, we must seek to find out the reason. I believe that we get a good many blessings just by asking; others we do not get, because there may be something in our life that needs to be brought to light.

When Daniel began to pray in Babylon for the deliverance of his people, he sought to find out what the trouble was, and why God had turned away His face from them. So there may be something in our life that is keeping back the blessing; if there is, we want to find it out. Someone, speaking on this subject, has said: "We are to ask with beggar's humility, to seek with a servant's carefulness, and to knock with the confidence of a friend."

RESPONDING IN PRAYER

"Lord, I want to wait expectantly for answers to prayer. Search my heart and show me if there is anything blocking my requests, and help me to change in order to please You."

Continuing in prayer . . .

How can you combine humility, carefulness, and confidence in terms of who you are in Christ as you go to prayer?

_____

_____

_____

_____

_____

_____

_____

_____

_____

SPIRITUAL GOALS FOR THE WEEK

_____

_____

_____

_____

_____

_____

_____

_____

_____

PROVED AND TRIED

$$\boxed{25}$$

He who calls you is faithful, who also will do it.
1 THESSALONIANS 5:24

*N*ow, my friends, bear in mind that God's Word is true, and it will help you wonderfully when you take up that Word of God to realize that every word of it is true. Infidels and skeptics will try to make you think it is not true. When they come to me and say that, I tell them, "Well, if you can get me a better Bible, I will give this up, but not until then." But when there is no book that will bear any comparison with it or touch it, why should we give it up? What has infidelity to give us in the place of it?

Bear in mind that these promises are all true. "He did not waver at the promise of God" (Romans 4:20). Abraham was fully persuaded that God was able to do what He had promised to do.

An old man told me that he had marked at all the promises of God the letters "P.T."—which stood for "Proved" and "Tried." None of the promises of God ever will or can fail. If you feed upon these promises, you will become rich in grace. There is no discount on any word God has ever said.

RESPONDING IN PRAYER

"Lord, give me the ability to study, meditate upon, and memorize Your promises under the wisdom and direction of the Holy Spirit."

Continuing in prayer . . .

_____

_____

_____

_____

_____

_____

_____

_____

What promises in your life have you found to be particularly tried and true? List them and ask God to continue to work them into your life.

_____

_____

_____

_____

_____

_____

_____

_____

_____

_____

SPIRITUAL GOALS FOR THE WEEK

_____

_____

_____

_____

_____

_____

_____

_____

_____

HIGHER THAN DUTY

26

We love Him because He first loved us.
1 JOHN 4:19

When we get to the higher plane of love, it will not be hard for us to work for the Lord. We will be glad to do anything, however small. God hates the great things in which love is not the motive power; but He delights in the little things that are prompted by a feeling of love. A cup of cold water given to a disciple in the spirit of love is of far more value in God's sight than the taking of a kingdom, done out of ambition and vainglory.

I am getting sick and tired of hearing the words *duty, duty.* You hear so many talk about it being the Christian's duty to do this and do that. My experience is that such Christians have very little success. Is there not a much higher platform than that of mere duty? Can we not engage in the service of Christ because we love Him? When that is the compelling power, it is so easy to work. It is not hard for a mother to watch over a sick child. She does not look upon it as any hardship.

You never hear Paul talking about what a hard time he had in his master's service. He was constrained by love to Christ, and by the love of Christ to him. He counted it a joy to labor, and even to suffer, for his blessed Master.

Perhaps you say I ought not to talk against duty, because a good deal of work would not be done at all if it were not from a sense of duty. But I want you to see what a poor, low motive that is, and how you may reach a higher plane of service.

RESPONDING IN PRAYER

"Lord, I know there is nothing wrong with duty, but please help my service for You stem from a higher motive of love, realizing that everything I do in Your name pleases You."

Continuing in prayer . . .

_____

_____

_____

_____

In today's world, even a sense of duty is no longer taught, but self-fulfillment instead. How can duty actually be put in a positive light?

_____

_____

_____

_____

_____

_____

_____

_____

_____

_____

SPIRITUAL GOALS FOR THE WEEK

_____

_____

_____

_____

_____

_____

_____

_____

_____

CLOTHED WITH COMPASSION

27

*For Adam and his wife the Lord God
made tunics of skin, and clothed them.*

GENESIS 3:21

*C*ertainly God could not have clothed Adam and Eve with the skins of beasts unless He had shed blood. It was a case of the innocent slain for the guilty. It may be that this was a type, away back in Eden, of Christ, the coming One, of the Sacrifice to be slain; and Adam might have said to his wife: "Well, even though God has driven us out of Eden, He loves us, and this coat is a token of His love."

Someone has said God put a lamp of promise into Adam's hand before He drove him out: "The seed of the woman shall bruise the head of the serpent." (See Genesis 3:15.)

To me it is a very sweet thought that sin was covered before Adam was driven out of Eden—that God dealt in grace with him before He dealt in judgment. Did you ever think what a terrible state of things it would be if man in his lost and ruined state were allowed to live forever? It was from love to Adam that God drove him out of Eden, that he should not live forever. God put the cherubim there with the flaming sword. But now Christ has come and taken the sword into His own bosom, and opened wide the gates, so that man can come in and eat. Adam might have been in Eden ten thousand years and then been led astray by Satan, but now our "life is hidden with Christ in God" (Colossians 3:3). Yes, man is safer with the Second Adam out of Eden than with the First Adam in Eden.

RESPONDING IN PRAYER

*"Lord, I appreciate the fact that You have not only
covered my sin in Christ, but You also will welcome me
to eat of the Tree of Life when I meet You in eternity."*

Continuing in prayer . . .

_____

_____

_____

_____

In what ways has God been gracious and compassionate to you even in the midst of your own folly and rebellion?

_____

_____

_____

_____

_____

_____

_____

_____

_____

SPIRITUAL GOALS FOR THE WEEK

_____

_____

_____

_____

_____

_____

_____

_____

THE FAR COUNTRY

---28---

And not many days after, the younger son gathered all together, journeyed to a far country, and there wasted his possession with prodigal living.

LUKE 15:13

*M*r. Spurgeon once summed up the things his audience had got over. Some, he said, had got over the prayers of faithful Sabbath-school teachers who used to weep over them and come to the house and talk to them. They resisted all their entreaties, and got over their influence. And some had got over their mother's tears and prayers, and she, perhaps, sleeps in the grace today. Some had got over the tears and prayers of their father and of their minister, who had prayed with them and wept with them. There was a time when the minister's sermons got right hold of them, but they have got over them now, and his sermons make no impression. Some had been through special meetings, and they have made no impression; they have not touched them. Still they say they are getting on.

Well, so they are; but bear in mind, they are getting on as fast as they can to hell, and there is not one man in ten thousand who can hope to be saved after he has grown so hard-hearted.

Oh, reader, if you are not already a child of God, safe bound for the Father's home, or if you are a wandering child, off in the far country, say, "I will arise" now! Let there be joy in heaven today over your return.

RESPONDING IN PRAYER

Lord, please move in the hearts of those I love and care about who are far away from you. Please bring them under the Lordship of Jesus Christ your Son."

Continuing in prayer . . .

_____

_____

_____

_____

_____

_____

How can you better pray for those unsaved or backslidden people that you might have influence upon?

_____

_____

_____

_____

_____

_____

_____

_____

_____

SPIRITUAL GOALS FOR THE WEEK

_____

_____

_____

_____

_____

_____

_____

WORDS OF WARNING

29

How shall we escape if we neglect so great a salvation?
HEBREWS 2:3

*Y*ou might have gone to Sodom and told the Sodomites that God was going to destroy Sodom, and they would have laughed at you, just as men make light of and laugh at hell. But did it change the fact? Did not God destroy the cities of the plain?

So with Jerusalem. Christ told how destruction would come upon it, and they mocked Him and crucified Him. But look down the stream of time! In forty short years, Titus came up against that city and besieged it, and there were a million that perished within it. Yes, those Jerusalem sinners can remember in the lost world tonight how Christ wept over Jerusalem, how He walked their streets, how He went into the temple and preached, and how He pleaded with them to escape for their lives, and to flee the damnation of hell; but they mocked on, they laughed on, they made light until it was too late, and they are gone now.

Oh, may God wake up this audience, and may every man and woman here escape for their lives before it is too late! "How shall we escape," says the apostle, "if we neglect so great a salvation?"

RESPONDING IN PRAYER

"Lord, how often I have ignored or even scoffed at Your warnings regarding my sin and yet You remain patient with me. Help me to be quick to repent."

Continuing in prayer . . .

_____

_____

_____

_____

_____

_____

_____

In what areas of your own life are you making light of God's conviction through the Holy Spirit? Confess these to God.

_____

_____

_____

_____

_____

_____

_____

_____

_____

_____

SPIRITUAL GOALS FOR THE WEEK

_____

_____

_____

_____

_____

_____

_____

_____

_____

PREFER ONE ANOTHER

30

"For he who is least among you all will be great."
LUKE 9:48

$\mathcal{S}$ome years ago I read a book that did me a great deal of good. It was entitled *The Training of the Twelve.* The writer said that Christ spent most of His time during the three years He was engaged publicly about His Father's business in training the twelve men. The training He gave them was very different from the training schools of the present day. The world teaches men that they must seek to be great; Christ taught that His disciples must be little; that in honor they must prefer one another; that they are not to be puffed up, not to harbor feelings of envy, but to be full of meekness and gentleness and lowliness of heart.

When an eminent painter was requested to paint Alexander the Great so as to give a perfect likeness of the Macedonian conqueror, he felt a difficulty. Alexander, in his wars, had been struck by a sword, and across his forehead was an immense scar. The painter said: "If I retain the scar, it will be an offense to the admirers of the monarch, and if I omit it, it will fail to be a perfect likeness. What shall I do?" He hit upon a happy expedient; he represented the emperor leaning upon his elbow, with his forefinger upon his brow, accidentally, as it seemed, covering the scar upon his forehead. Might not we represent each other with the finger of charity upon the scar, instead of representing the scar deeper and blacker than it really is? Christians may learn even from heathendom a lesson of charity, of human kindness and of love.

RESPONDING IN PRAYER

"Lord, help me to overlook the scars and flaws of others and see Your image in them and love for them. For those that seem better than I, help me not to be envious or jealous, but learn from them."

Continuing in prayer . . . _____

_____

_____

_____

_____

As you seek to excel and do your best, do you ever seek to be above or greater than others? Ask God to deal with this subtle temptation.

_____

_____

_____

_____

_____

_____

_____

_____

_____

SPIRITUAL GOALS FOR THE WEEK

_____

_____

_____

_____

_____

_____

_____

_____

_____

CONFESSING CHRIST

———————— 31 ————————

*"And whoever does not bear his cross and
come after Me cannot be My disciple."*

LUKE 14:27

We can afford to suffer with Him a little while if we are going to reign with Him forever. We can afford to take up our cross and follow Him, to be despised and rejected by the world, with such a bright prospect in view. If the glories of heaven are real, it will be to His praise and to our advantage to share in His rejection now.

May the Lord keep us from halting; and may we, when weighed in the balance, not be found wanting! May God help every reader to do all that the poor blind beggar did, and all that Joseph of Arimathea did! Let us confess Him at all times and in all places. Let us show our friends that we are out and out on His side.

Everyone has a circle that he can influence, and God will hold us responsible for the influence we possess. Joseph of Arimathea and the blind man had circles in which their influence was powerful. I can influence people that others cannot reach; and they, in their turn, can reach a class that I could not touch. It is only for a little while that we can confess Him and work for Him. It is only for a few months or years; and then the eternal ages will roll on, and great will be our reward in the crowning day that is coming. We shall then hear the Master say to us: "Well done, good and faithful servant; you were faithful over a few things, I will make you ruler over many things. Enter into the joy of your lord" (Matthews 25:21).

God grant it may be so!

RESPONDING IN PRAYER

*"Lord, I know that through Your calling I have influence
in the lives of those around me. Help me to use it
to persuade others by the way I live for Christ."*

Continuing in prayer . . .

_____

_____

_____

_____

_____

What are your strengths and gifts that positively influence others? How can they be turned into a witness for Christ?

_____

_____

_____

_____

_____

_____

_____

_____

_____

_____

SPIRITUAL GOALS FOR THE WEEK

_____

_____

_____

_____

_____

_____

_____

_____

A LEGACY OF PEACE

32

So Jesus said to them again, "Peace to you!
As the Father has sent Me, I also send you."

JOHN 20:21

$\mathcal{D}$id you ever think that when Christ was dying on the cross, He made a will?
Perhaps you have thought that no one ever remembered you in a will. If you are
in the kingdom, Christ remembered you in His. He willed His body to Joseph of
Arimathea; He willed His mother to John, the son of Zebedee; and He willed His
Spirit back to His Father. But to His disciples He said, "My peace, I leave that
with you; that is my legacy. My joy, I give that to you." "My joy"—think of it.
"My peace"—not our peace, but His peace!

They say a man can't make a will now that lawyers can't break. I will challenge them to break Christ's will; let them try it. No judge or jury can set that
aside. Christ rose to execute His own will. If He had left us a lot of gold, thieves
would have stolen it in the first century; but He left His peace and His joy for
every true believer, and no power on earth can take it from him who trusts.

A great many people are trying to make their peace with God, but that has
already been done. God has not left it for us to do; all that we have to do is to
enter into it, to accept it.

RESPONDING IN PRAYER

"Lord, Your peace and joy are a gift to me.
Thank You for leaving them to me to enjoy forever."

Continuing in prayer . . .

_____

_____

_____

_____

_____

_____

_____

How would you describe both the peace and joy that you have experienced as a legacy from God? How can you be assured it is yours?

_____

_____

_____

_____

_____

_____

_____

_____

_____

_____

SPIRITUAL GOALS FOR THE WEEK

_____

_____

_____

_____

_____

_____

_____

_____

_____

_____

PEOPLE OF FAITH

33

These all died in faith, not having received the promises,
but having seen them afar off were assured of them, embraced them.
HEBREWS 11:13

In Hebrews 11 the writer brings up one person after another, and each was a man or a woman of faith; they made the world better by living in it. Listen to this description of what was accomplished by these men and women of faith: "Who through faith subdued kingdoms, worked righteousness, obtained promises, stopped the mouths of lions, quenched the violence of fire, escaped the edge of the sword, out of weakness were made strong, became valiant in battle, turned to flight the armies of the aliens. . . . They were stoned, they were sawn in two, were tempted, were slain with the sword. They wandered about in sheepskins and goatskins, being destitute, afflicted, tormented—of whom the world was not worthy. They wandered in deserts and mountains, in dens and caves of the earth. And these all, having obtained a good testimony through faith, did not receive the promise, God having provided something better for us, that they should not be made perfect apart from us" (verses 33–34, 37–40).

Surely no child of God can read these words without being stirred. It is said that "women received their dead raised to life again" (Hebrews 11:35). Many of you have children who have gone far astray and have been taken captive by strong drink, or led away by their lusts and passions; and you have become greatly discouraged about them. But if you have faith in God, they may be raised up as from the dead and brought back again. The wanderers may be reclaimed; the drunkards and harlots may be reached and saved. There is no man or woman, however low he or she may have sunk, but can be reached.

RESPONDING IN PRAYER

"Lord, I sometimes think of these great exploits of faith as only
fit for super saints, but these better things are also promised to me.
Grant me the faith to take hold of them."

Continuing in prayer . . .

_____

_____

_____

FOR REFLECTION

What would you like to accomplish by faith in this life that to you may seem as difficult as some of the above exploits? Ask God to increase your faith, wisdom, and finally, obedience.

_____

_____

_____

_____

_____

_____

_____

_____

_____

SPIRITUAL GOALS FOR THE WEEK

_____

_____

_____

_____

_____

_____

_____

_____

A LEAP OF FAITH

34

Casting all your care upon Him, for He cares for you.
1 PETER 5:7

I was standing with a friend at his garden gate one evening when two little children came by. As they approached us, he said to me, "Watch the difference in these two boys."

Taking one of them in his arms, he stood him on the gatepost, and stepping back a few feet, he folded his arms and called to the little fellow to jump. In an instant, the boy sprang toward him and was caught in his arms. Then turning to the second boy, he tried the same experiment. But in the second case it was different. The child trembled and refused to move. My friend held out his arms and tried to induce the child to trust in his strength, but nothing could move him. At last my friend had to lift him down from the post and let him go.

"What makes such a difference in the two?" I asked. My friend smiled and said, "The first is my own boy and knows me; the other is a stranger's child whom I have never seen before."

There was all the difference. My friend was equally able to prevent both from falling, but the difference was in the boys themselves. The first had assurance in his father's ability and acted upon it, while the second, although he might have believed in the ability to save him from harm, would not put his belief into action.

So it is with us. We hesitate to trust ourselves to that loving One whose plans for us are far higher than any we have ourselves made. He, too, with outstretched arms, calls us, and would we but listen to His voice we would hear that invitation and promise of assurance as He gave it of old: "Come to Me, all you who labor and are heavy laden, and I will give you rest" (Matthew 11:28).

RESPONDING IN PRAYER

"Lord, I first need to give You my burdens and fears so as to enter into Your rest. Then give me the assurance to trust You by stepping out into life's challenges, knowing that You are with me."

Continuing in prayer . . .

_____

_____

_____

Do you sometimes forget that God has better plans for you than you could construct? Seek Him for a better way to plug into His plans.

_____

_____

_____

_____

_____

_____

_____

_____

_____

_____

SPIRITUAL GOALS FOR THE WEEK

_____

_____

_____

_____

_____

_____

_____

_____

_____

POWER IN THE BLOOD

---35---

And I said to him, "Sir, you know." So he said to me,
"These are the ones who come out of the great tribulation, and washed
their robes and made them white in the blood of the Lamb."
REVELATION 7:14

May God help us to make much of the blood of His Son. It cost God so much to give us His Son, and shall we try to keep Him from the world that is perishing from the want of Him? The world can get along without us, but not without Christ. Let us preach Christ in season and out of season. Let us go to the sick and dying, and hold up the Savior who came to seek and save them—who died to redeem them.

Once more, in Revelation 7:14, "These are the ones who come out of the great tribulation, and washed their robes and made them white in the blood of the Lamb." Sinner, how are you going to get your robes clean if you do not get them washed in the blood of the Lamb? How are you going to wash them? Can you make them clean?

I pray that at last we may all get back to the paradise above. There they are singing the sweet song of redemption. May it be the happy lot of each of us to join them. It will be a few years at the longest before we shall be there to sing the sweet song of Moses and the Lamb. But if you die without Christ, without hope and without God, where will you be? Oh, sinner, be wise; do not make light of the blood.

An aged minister of the Gospel, on his dying bed, said, "Bring me the Bible." Putting his finger upon the verse "The blood of Jesus Christ his Son cleanseth us from all sin" (1 John 1:7 KJV), he said, "I die in the hope of this verse." It was not his fifty years' preaching but the blood of Christ. May God grant that when we come at last to stand before His throne, our robes may be washed in the cleansing blood of Christ!

RESPONDING IN PRAYER

"Lord, forgive me for not having enough faith in the power of Your
blood to cleanse me completely in all circumstances and allow me
to walk in victory over all my adversaries. Apply it to me now."

Continuing in prayer . . .

FOR REFLECTION

Search your heart for past sins that have not been confessed. Ask God to cleanse you by His blood and in the future bring to mind the remembrance of His blood.

_____

_____

_____

_____

_____

_____

_____

_____

_____

_____

_____

SPIRITUAL GOALS FOR THE WEEK

_____

_____

_____

_____

_____

_____

_____

_____

FALSE GODS

------- |36| -------

*"No one can serve two masters; for either he will hate the one
and love the other, or else he will be loyal to the one and
despise the other. You cannot serve God and mammon."*

MATTHEW 6:24

*M*ark you, He did not say—"No one *shall* serve . . . You *shall* not serve . . . ,"
but "No one *can* serve . . . You *cannot* serve. . . ." That means more than a com-
mand; it means that you cannot mix the worship of the true God with the worship of another god any more than you can mix oil and water. It cannot be done.
There is not room for any other throne in the heart if Christ is there. If worldli-
ness shall come in, godliness would go out.

The road to heaven and the road to hell lead in different directions. Which
master will you choose to follow? Be an out-and-out Christian. "Him only shalt
thou serve." Only thus can you be well-pleasing to God. The Jews were punished
with seventy years of captivity because they worshiped false gods. They have suffered nearly nineteen hundred years because they rejected the Messiah. Will you
incur God's displeasure by rejecting Christ too? He died to save you. Trust Him
with your whole heart, for with the heart man believeth unto righteousness.

I believe that when Christ has the first place in our hearts—when the kingdom of God is first in everything—we shall have power, and we shall not have
power until we give Him His rightful place. If we let one false god come in and
steal our love away from the God of heaven, we shall not have peace or power.

RESPONDING IN PRAYER

*"Lord, there are still areas in my life where the kingdom of God
is not the priority. Show me how Your kingdom enters in
or show me how to change my behavior."*

Continuing in prayer . . .

_____

_____

_____

_____

_____

There are many different ways money can play an inappropriate role in your life.
Name as many as you can, even if some have opposite effects.

_____

_____

_____

_____

_____

_____

_____

_____

_____

_____

SPIRITUAL GOALS FOR THE WEEK

_____

_____

_____

_____

_____

_____

_____

_____

WHO AM I?

"Or what woman, having ten silver coins, if she loses one coin, does not light a lamp, sweep the house, and search carefully until she finds it?"
LUKE 15:8

*W*here art thou?" A man said to me: "How do you know that God put that question to Adam?"

The best answer I can give is, because He has put it to me many a time. I doubt whether there ever has been a son or a daughter of Adam who has not heard that voice ringing through his soul many a time. Who am I? What am I? Where am I going? So let us put the question to ourselves personally: "Where am I?"—not in the sight of man; that is of very little account; but where am I in the sight of God?

Adam ought to have been the first seeker. Adam ought to have gone up and down Eden crying: "My God, my God, where art Thou? I have sinned. I have fallen."

But God, then as now, took the place of the seeker. No man, from the time that Adam fell, down to the present hour, ever thought of seeking God until God first sought for him. "The Son of man is come to seek and to save that which was lost" (Luke 19:10 KJV). I believe that the Son of Man who uttered those words is the same whose voice was heard back there in Eden, "Adam, where art thou?" For six thousand years God has been seeking for man.

In the fifteenth chapter of Luke, there are three parables just to teach us that God is the seeker. It was not the sheep that was seeking the shepherd; it was the shepherd going out into the desert to hunt until he found the lost sheep. It was not that piece of silver seeking the woman; it was the woman seeking for the lost piece of silver. Those parables are given to teach us that God is the great seeker.

RESPONDING IN PRAYER

"Lord, how often I hide from Your presence when I sin. Help me to realize Your immediate forgiveness and see myself not just as fallen but truly restored through the work of Your Son Jesus Christ."

Continuing in prayer . . .

In what ways do you usually hide from God when you have sinned, are angry, depressed, etc.? Ask God how He would want you to face these "escape routes" and run into His arms.

_____

_____

_____

_____

_____

_____

_____

_____

_____

SPIRITUAL GOALS FOR THE WEEK

_____

_____

_____

_____

_____

_____

_____

_____

THE BIRDS OVERHEAD

—————|38|—————

*Above all, taking the shield of faith, with which you will
be able to quench all the fiery darts of the wicked one.*

EPHESIANS 6:16

If resisting the Spirit of God is an unpardonable sin, then we have all committed it, and there is no hope for any of us; for I do not believe there is a minister
or a worker in Christ's vineyard who has not, sometime in his life, resisted the
Holy Spirit, who has not sometime in his life rejected the Spirit of God. To resist
the Holy Spirit is one thing, and to commit that awful sin of blasphemy against
the Holy Spirit is another thing; and we want to take the Scripture and just com-
pare them. Now, some people say, "I have such blasphemous thoughts; there are
some awful thoughts that come into my mind against God," and they think that is
the unpardonable sin. We are not to blame for having bad thoughts come into our
minds. If we harbor them, then we are to blame. But if the devil comes and darts
an evil thought into my mind, and I say, "Lord, help me," sin is not reckoned to
me. Who has not had evil thoughts flash into his mind, flash into his heart, and
been called to fight them?

One old divine says, "You are not to blame for the birds that fly over your
head, but if you allow them to come down and make a nest in your hair, then
you are to blame. You are to blame if you don't fight them off." And so with these
evil thoughts that come flashing into our minds; we have to fight them. We are
not to harbor them; we are not to entertain them. Remember, when an evil
thought or desire comes into your mind, it is no sign that you have committed
the unpardonable sin.

RESPONDING IN PRAYER

*"Lord, too often I do not fight evil thoughts from the very beginning
but entertain them, and then it is too late. Don't let me compound
this by believing that I cannot be forgiven as well."*

Continuing in prayer . . .

_____

_____

_____

_____

Think back on your life and write down what, from your perspective, was the worst sin that you ever committed. Do you truly believe God has forgiven and forgotten? Entrust the "smaller" sins with confidence to Him as well.

_____

_____

_____

_____

_____

_____

_____

_____

SPIRITUAL GOALS FOR THE WEEK

_____

_____

_____

_____

_____

_____

OVERCOMING THE WORLD

| 39 |
---

*For whatever is born of God overcomes the world. And this is the victory
that has overcome the world—our faith. Who is he who overcomes
the world, but he who believes that Jesus is the Son of God?*

1 JOHN 5:4–5

*F*or everything in the world—the cravings of sinful man, the lust of his eyes
and the boasting of what he has and does—comes not from the Father but from
the world. "And the world is passing away, and the lust of it; but he who does the
will of God abides forever" (1 John 2:17).

"The world" does not mean nature around us. God nowhere tells us that the
material world is an enemy to be overcome. On the contrary, we read: "The earth
is the Lord's, and all its fullness, the world and those who dwell therein." The
psalmist also writes, "The heavens declare the glory of God; and the firmament
shows His handiwork."

"The world" means "human life and society that is alienated from God,
through being centered on material aims and objects, and thus it opposes God's
Spirit and kingdom." Christ told His disciples and tells us, "If the world hates you,
you know that it hated Me before it hated you" (John 15:18).

Love of the world means the forgetfulness of the eternal future by reason of
love for passing things.

How can the world be overcome? Not by education, not by experience; only
by faith. "This is the victory that has overcome the world—our faith. Who is he
who overcomes the world, but he who believes that Jesus is the Son of God?"

RESPONDING IN PRAYER

*"Lord, I admit that in many respects I am attached to the world and
don't hate it like I should. Help my faith in You, and the eternal
kingdom I see by faith, to overcome the world."*

Continuing in prayer . . .

_____

_____

_____

How can you move from love, or at best, neutrality, to hating the things that of-fend God and rebel against His rule?

_____

_____

_____

_____

_____

_____

_____

_____

_____

SPIRITUAL GOALS FOR THE WEEK

_____

_____

_____

_____

_____

_____

_____

_____

HUMILITY AND FRUIT

───────── 40 ─────────

Likewise you younger people, submit yourselves to your elders. Yes, all of
you be submissive to one another, and be clothed with humility, for
"God resists the proud, but gives grace to the humble."

1 PETER 5:5

A man can counterfeit love, he can counterfeit faith, he can counterfeit hope and all the other graces; but it is very difficult to counterfeit humility. You soon detect mock humility. They have a saying in the East among the Arabs that as the tares and the wheat grow they show which God has blessed. The ears of wheat that God has blessed bow their heads and acknowledge every grain, and the more fruitful they are, the lower their heads are bowed. The tares, which God has sent as a curse, lift up their heads erect, high above the wheat, but they are only fruitful of evil.

I have a pear tree on my farm that is very beautiful; it appears to be one of the most beautiful trees on my place. Every branch seems to be reaching up to the light and stands almost like a wax candle, but I never get any fruit from it. I have another tree, which was so full of fruit last year that the branches almost touched the ground. If we only get down low enough, my friends, God will use every one of us to His glory.

"As the lark that soars the highest builds her nest the lowest; as the nightingale that sings so sweetly sings in the shade when all things rest; as the branches that are most laden with fruit bend lowest; as the ship most laden sinks deepest in the water; so the holiest Christians are the humblest."

RESPONDING IN PRAYER

"Lord, bring me low before You so that my fruit can hang low
in its abundance. Give me the example of Jesus, the greatest
One to live on earth, and yet the most humble."

Continuing in prayer . . .

_____

_____

_____

_____

_____

When has a lack of humility, even in the form of self-sufficiency, kept you from bearing fruit? How can you better remember that without Christ you can do nothing?

_____

_____

_____

_____

_____

_____

_____

_____

_____

SPIRITUAL GOALS FOR THE WEEK

_____

_____

_____

_____

_____

_____

_____

Poor for Our Sake

------------------ 41 ------------------

For you know the grace of our Lord Jesus Christ, that though He was rich,
yet for your sakes He became poor, that you through His poverty might
become rich.

2 CORINTHIANS 8:9

*D*o you want to know how you can reach the masses? Go to their homes and enter into sympathy with them. Tell them you have come to do them good, and let them see that you have a heart to feel for them. When they find out that you really love them, all those things that are in their hearts against God and against Christianity will be swept out of the way. Atheists may tell them that you only want to get their money and that you do not really care for their happiness. We have to contradict that lie by our lives and send it back to the pit where it came from.

We are not going to do it unless we go personally to them and prove that we really love them. There are thousands of families that could easily be reached if we had thousands of Christians going to them and entering into sympathy with their sorrows. That is what they want. This poor world is groaning and sighing for sympathy—human sympathy. I am quite sure it was that in Christ's life that touched the hearts of the common people. He made Himself one of them. He who was rich for our sakes became poor. He was born in the manger so that He might put Himself on a level with the lowest of the low.

I think that in this manner He teaches His disciples a lesson. He wants us to convince that world that He is their friend. They do not believe it. If once the world were to grasp this thought, that Jesus Christ is the friend of the sinner, they would soon flock to Him.

RESPONDING IN PRAYER

"Lord, do I put my own concern for the poor into action
by serving them, or is it mere sentiment and some spare change?
Help me to get involved with my hands as well as my head."

Continuing in prayer . . .

_____

_____

_____

_____

Choose one project that you can commit to that will bless the poor or disadvantaged in a tangible way. Discuss it with the Lord.

_____

_____

_____

_____

_____

_____

_____

_____

_____

SPIRITUAL GOALS FOR THE WEEK

_____

_____

_____

_____

_____

_____

_____

_____

_____

IN A FAR COUNTRY

---42---

"Your own wickedness will correct you, and your backslidings
will rebuke you. Know therefore and see that it is an evil and bitter
thing that you have forsaken the Lord your God, and the fear of Me
is not in you," says the Lord God of hosts.
JEREMIAH 2:19

I do not exaggerate when I say that I have seen hundreds of backsliders come back, and I have asked them if they have not found it an evil and a bitter thing to leave the Lord. You cannot find a real backslider who has known the Lord but will admit that it is an evil and a bitter thing to turn away from Him. I do not know of any one verse more used to bring back wanderers than that very one. May it bring *you* back if you have wandered into the far country.

Look at Lot. Did he not find it an evil and a bitter thing? He was twenty years in Sodom and never made a convert. He got on well in the sight of the world. Men would have told you that he was one of the most influential and worthy men in all Sodom. But alas! He ruined his family. And it is a pitiful thing to see that old backslider going through the streets of Sodom at midnight, after he has warned his children and they have turned a deaf ear.

I have never known a man and his wife to backslide without its proving utter ruin to their children. They will make a mockery of religion and will deride their parents: "Your own wickedness will correct you, and your backslidings will rebuke you." Did not David find it so? Mark him, crying, "O my son Absalom—my son, my son Absalom—if only I had died in your place! O Absalom my son, my son!" I think it was the ruin, rather than the death, of his son that caused this anguish.

RESPONDING IN PRAYER

"Lord, keep me from a subtle form of backsliding which is a neglect of
my spiritual duties and a lukewarm spirit. Give me a passion to
worship, obey, and serve You diligently."

Continuing in prayer . . .

_____

_____

_____

_____

What areas of your spiritual walk might you be neglecting or performing in a half-hearted manner? Ask God to strengthen you and give you a greater desire for Him.

_____

_____

_____

_____

_____

_____

_____

_____

_____

SPIRITUAL GOALS FOR THE WEEK

_____

_____

_____

_____

_____

_____

_____

_____

_____

_____

_____

NO FEAR

| 43 |

For you died, and your life is hidden with Christ in God.
COLOSSIANS 3:3

A great many young disciples are afraid they will remain in their faith, "He who keeps Israel shall neither slumber nor sleep" (Psalm 121:4). It is the work of Christ to keep us; and if He keeps us there will be no danger of our falling.

We have no strength in ourselves. We are no match for Satan; he has had six thousand years' experience. But then we remember that the One who neither slumbers nor sleeps is our keeper. In Isaiah 41:10, we read, "Fear not, for I am with you; be not dismayed, for I am your God. I will strengthen you, yes, I will help you, I will uphold you with My righteous right hand." In Jude also, we are told that He is "able to keep [us] from stumbling" (verse 24).

But Christ is something more. He is our Shepherd. It is the work of a shepherd to care for the sheep, to feed them and protect them. "I am the good shepherd. . . . I lay down My life for the sheep" (John 10:14–15). In that wonderful tenth chapter of John, Christ uses the personal pronoun no less than twenty-eight times, in declaring what He is and what He will do. In verse 28 he says, "They shall never perish, neither shall any *man* pluck them out of my hand" (KJV). But notice the word *man* is in italics. See how the verse really reads: "Neither shall any pluck them out of my hand." No devil or man shall be able to do it. In another place the Scripture declares, "Your life is hidden with Christ in God" (Colossians 3:3). How safe and how secure!

RESPONDING IN PRAYER

"Lord, with the pressures of this life I sometimes worry about persevering in the long run. I thank You that nothing and no one can take me away from You. Hold me close during life's trials."

Continuing in prayer . . .

_____

_____

_____

_____

_____

Describe the feeling of being abandoned by God during trials or times of dryness. Express to God your deep desire to stay faithful even during times when you don't understand what He is doing.

_____

_____

_____

_____

_____

_____

_____

_____

_____

_____

SPIRITUAL GOALS FOR THE WEEK

_____

_____

_____

_____

_____

_____

_____

_____

_____

_____

THE OLD AND THE NEW

───────┤44├───────

Knowing this first, that no prophecy of Scripture
is of any private interpretation.

2 PETER 1:20

In the gospel of Matthew, there are more than a hundred quotations from twenty of the books in the Old Testament. In the gospel of Mark, there are fifteen quotations taken from thirteen of the books. In the gospel of Luke, there are thirty-four quotations from thirteen books. In the gospel of John, there are eleven quotations from six books. In the four Gospels alone, there are more than 160 quotations from the Old Testament.

You sometimes hear men saying they do not believe all the Bible, but they believe the teaching of Jesus Christ in the four gospels. Well, if I believe that, I have to accept these 160 quotations from the Old Testament. In Paul's letters to the Corinthians, there are 53 quotations from the Old Testament; sometimes he takes whole paragraphs from it. In Hebrews, there are 85 quotations—in that one book of 13 chapters. In Galatians, 16 quotations. In the book of Revelation alone, there are 245 quotations and allusions.

A great many want to throw out the Old Testament. It is good historic reading, they say, but they don't believe that it is a part of the Word of God and don't regard it as essential in the scheme of salvation. The last letter Paul wrote contained the following words: "And that from childhood you have known the Holy Scriptures, which are able to make you wise for salvation through faith which is in Christ Jesus." All the Scriptures that the apostles possessed were the Old Testament.

RESPONDING IN PRAYER

"Lord, grant me a deeper understanding of the Old Testament
and especially how it interrelates with the New Testament.
Help me to see Christ more clearly throughout Your Word."

Continuing in prayer . . .

_____

_____

_____

_____

What are your favorite representations of Christ from the Old Testament? How do you best see the New Testament as the Old's fulfillment?

_____

_____

_____

_____

_____

_____

_____

_____

_____

SPIRITUAL GOALS FOR THE WEEK

_____

_____

_____

_____

_____

_____

_____

_____

GLORY BEFORE US

─────── 45 ───────

And when the Chief Shepherd appears, you will receive
the crown of glory that does not fade away.
1 PETER 5:4

*T*here is no peace until we see the finished work of Jesus Christ—until we can look back and see the cross of Christ between us and our sins. When we see that Jesus was "the end of the law for righteousness," that He "tasted death for every man," that He "suffered . . . the just for the unjust," then comes peace. Then there is "this grace in which we stand." There is plenty of grace for us as we need it— day by day, and hour by hour.

Then there is glory for the time to come. A great many people seem to forget that the best is before us. Dr. Bonar says that everything before the true believer is "glorious." This thought took hold of my soul, and I began to look the matter up and see what I could find in Scripture that was glorious hereafter. I found that the kingdom we are going to inherit is glorious; our crown is to be a "crown of glory"; the city we are going to inhabit is the city of the glorified; the songs we are to sing are the songs of the glorified; we are to wear garments of "glory and beauty." Furthermore, our society will be the society of the glorified; our rest is to be "glorious"; the country to which we are going is to be full of "the glory of God and of the Lamb."

Many are always looking on the backward path and mourning over the troubles through which they have passed. They keep lugging up the cares and anxieties they have been called on to bear and are forever looking at them. Why should we go reeling and staggering under the burdens and cares of life when we have such prospects before us?

RESPONDING IN PRAYER

"Lord, help me not to live life looking in the rearview mirror but looking forward to the crown of glory in Your city of glory. May I do all to enhance Your glory through the gifts You have given me."

Continuing in prayer . . .

_____

_____

_____

_____

What burdens or cares seem to prevent you from looking forward? How can you give those to God, trusting that He will set you free to focus on the glory ahead?

_____

_____

_____

_____

_____

_____

_____

_____

_____

SPIRITUAL GOALS FOR THE WEEK

_____

_____

_____

_____

_____

_____

_____

_____

_____

UNIVERSAL LAWS

The law of the Lord is perfect, converting the soul; the testimony of the Lord is sure, making wise the simple; the statutes of the Lord are right, rejoicing the heart; the commandment of the Lord is pure, enlightening the eyes.

PSALM 19:7–8

Now men may dispute as much as they joke about other parts of the Bible, but I have never met an honest man who found fault with the Ten Commandments. Infidels may mock the Lawgiver and reject Him who has delivered us from the curse of the law, but they can't help admitting that the commandments are right. Renan said that they are for all nations and will remain the commandments of God during all the centuries.

If God created this world, He must make some laws to govern it. In order to make life safe, we must have good laws; there is not a country the sun shines upon that does not possess laws. Now this is God's law. It has come from on high, and infidels and skeptics have to admit that it is pure. Legislatures nearly all over the world adopt it as the foundation of their legal systems.

Now the question for you and me is: Are we keeping these commandments? If God made us, as we know He did, He had a right to make that law; and if we don't use it rightly, it would have been better for us if we had never had it, for it will condemn us. We are found wanting. And being found condemned, we have only one hope for deliverance—Jesus Christ the righteous.

RESPONDING IN PRAYER

"Lord, help me to review the Ten Commandments and use it as a part of my soul-searching before You. I want to respect and love Your law above all things."

Continuing in prayer . . .

_____

_____

_____

_____

_____

_____

FOR REFLECTION

Ask the Lord to give you new incentives to keep His commands where you are weakest. Remember that we are not under the curse of the law but under grace.

_____

_____

_____

_____

_____

_____

_____

_____

_____

_____

SPIRITUAL GOALS FOR THE WEEK

_____

_____

_____

_____

_____

_____

_____

_____

_____

_____

Our Parents' Love

---[47]---

Honor your father and your mother, as the Lord your God has commanded you, that your days may be long, and that it may be well with you in the land which the Lord your God is giving you.

DEUTERONOMY 5:16

It would be easy to multiply texts from the Bible to prove this truth. Obedience and respect at home prepare the way of obedience to the employer, and they are joined with other virtues that help toward a prosperous career, crowned with a ripe, honored old age. Disobedience and disrespect for parents are often the first steps in the downward track. Many a criminal has testified that this is the point where he first went astray. I have lived over sixty years, and I have learned one thing if I have learned nothing else—that no man or woman who dishonors father or mother ever prospers.

Young man, young woman, how do you treat your parents? Tell me that, and I will tell you how you are going to get on in life. When I hear a young man speaking contemptuously of his gray-haired father or mother, I say he has sunk very low indeed. When I see a young man as polite as any gentleman can be when he is out in society, but who snaps at his mother and speaks unkindly to his father, I would not give the snap of my fingers for his religion.

If there is any man or woman on earth who ought to be treated kindly and tenderly, it is that loving mother or that loving father. If they cannot have your regard through life, what reward are they to have for all their care and anxiety? Think how they loved you and provided for you in your early days.

RESPONDING IN PRAYER

"Lord, I want to truly honor my parents in a way that is pleasing to You. Help me to give back to them a fraction of what they have given to me, that I might brighten up their lives."

Continuing in prayer . . .

_____

_____

_____

_____

Are there any barriers between you and your parents? What can you do to show greater appreciation for what they have done in your life?

_____

_____

_____

_____

_____

_____

_____

_____

_____

SPIRITUAL GOALS FOR THE WEEK

_____

_____

_____

_____

_____

_____

_____

SOWING TO THE FLESH

---|48|---

*"And if your foot causes you to sin, cut it off. It is better for you
to enter life lame, than having two feet, to be cast into hell."*
MARK 9:45

*N*o matter how painful it may be, break with sin at once. Severe operations are
often necessary, for the skillful surgeon knows that the disease cannot be cured by
surface applications. The farmer takes his hoe and his spade and his axe, and he
cuts away the obnoxious growths and burns the roots out of the ground with fire.

If your right eye offend you, pluck it out, as Christ says, and cast it away, for it
is better for you "that one of your members perish than for your whole body to
be cast into hell. And if your right hand causes you to sin, cut it off and cast it from
you . . . [rather] than for your whole body to be cast into hell" (Matthew 5:29–30).

Remember that the tares and the wheat will be separated at the judgment day,
if not before. Sowing to the flesh and sowing to the Spirit inevitably lead in diverg-
ing paths. The axe will be "laid to the root of the trees . . . [and] every tree which
does not bear good fruit [will be] cut down and thrown into the fire" (Matthew
3:10). The threshing floor will be thoroughly purged, and the wheat will be gathered into the garner, while the chaff will be burned with unquenchable fire.

Beware your habits. A recent writer has said: "Could the young but realize how
soon they will become mere walking bundles of habits, they would give more heed
to their conduct while in the plastic state." We are spinning our own fates, good or
evil, and never to be undone. Every smallest stroke of virtue or of vice leaves its
ever-so-little scar. The drunken Rip Van Winkle, in Irving's story, excuses himself for
every fresh dereliction by saying, "I won't count this time." Well, he may not count
it, but it is being counted nonetheless.

RESPONDING IN PRAYER

*"Lord, help me not only to be aware of the destructive power of sin,
but that anything in my life that doesn't bear good fruit will count
for nothing. Please multiply my fruit for Your name's sake."*

Continuing in prayer . . .

_____

_____

_____

What areas of your life might need radical surgery or at least pruning? Admit to God that you want to bear fruit but you will allow Him to do this first.

_____

_____

_____

_____

_____

_____

_____

_____

_____

_____

SPIRITUAL GOALS FOR THE WEEK

_____

_____

_____

_____

_____

_____

_____

_____

RAISED IN GLORY

---49---

He who has the Son has life;
he who does not have the Son of God does not have life.
1 JOHN 5:12

℘ather, I desire that they also whom You gave Me, may be with Me where I am; that they may behold My glory, which You have given Me." This is Christ's prayer.

Now when a man believes on the Lord Jesus Christ, he receives eternal life. A great many people make a mistake right there. The apostle John said that the person who believes on the Son has, *has* eternal life. John did not say that the person shall have it when he comes to die; it is in the present tense; it is mine now—if I believe. It is the gift of God; that is enough. You cannot bury the gift of God; you cannot bury eternal life. All the gravediggers in the world cannot dig a grave large enough and deep enough to hold eternal life; all the coffin-makers in the world cannot make a coffin large enough and strong enough to hold eternal life; it is mine. It *is* mine!

When Paul said "to be absent from the body and to be present with the Lord" (2 Corinthians 5:8), he meant what he said: that he was not going to be separated from Him for years and years. The Spirit that was given him when he was converted he had from a new life and a new nature, and they could not lay that away in the sepulcher. Even the body shall be raised. This body, sown in dishonor, shall be raised in glory; this body that has known corruption shall put on immortality. It is only a question of time.

RESPONDING IN PRAYER

"Lord, eternal life when we are still earthbound is a hard concept to grasp. Give me a greater understanding of it in my mind, heart, and soul—by faith. Let me cherish it like nothing else I possess."

Continuing in prayer . . .

_____

_____

_____

_____

_____

How do you explain eternal life with God to an unbeliever or someone seeking God? Ask God for a clearer understanding and experience of it in your own life as well.

_____

_____

_____

_____

_____

_____

_____

_____

_____

SPIRITUAL GOALS FOR THE WEEK

_____

_____

_____

_____

_____

_____

_____

_____

A PRECIOUS ANOINTING

---|50|---

And behold, a woman in the city who was a sinner, when she knew that Jesus sat at the table in the Pharisee's house, brought an alabaster flask of fragrant oil, and stood at His feet behind Him weeping; and she began to wash His feet with her tears, and wiped them with the hair of her head; and she kissed His feet and anointed them with the fragrant oil.

LUKE 7:37–38

*I*n the seventh chapter of Luke we read of a poor woman who came with an alabaster box and anointed the Lord with ointment, and in the twelfth chapter of John Mary also takes a box and breaks it and pours out the precious ointment upon Him.

When Mary broke that box and anointed Jesus, there was a great indignation among the disciples. Judas, that traitor, who was already planning to sell his Lord, was the most indignant of all. He was treasurer of the company.

It was a great thing when Samuel anointed David, but no king ever had such a kingly anointing as when Mary anointed Christ with that ointment that was so sweet and so precious. Judas figured up the price and said that it was worth three hundred denarii! A denarius would hire a man all day, so that one pound of ointment had cost a year's work.

But Jesus estimated the worth differently. He rebuked the disciples, and said: "Why do you trouble the woman? For she has done a good work for Me. . . . For in pouring this fragrant oil on My body, she did it for My burial. Assuredly, I say to you, wherever this gospel is preached in the whole world, what this woman has done will also be told as a memorial to her."

Think of it! Wherever the gospel of the Son of God is to be preached in this wide world, that story is to be told! There is nothing lost that we do for Christ.

RESPONDING IN PRAYER

"Lord, help me to remember that I too need to have this attitude of repentance as well as joy when I think of what You have done for me. May I now share this joy by proclaiming Your Gospel."

Continuing in prayer . . .

Nothing is lost in what you do for Christ. Pray for God's anointing in your own life to do things both great and small.

_____

_____

_____

_____

_____

_____

_____

_____

_____

_____

SPIRITUAL GOALS FOR THE WEEK

_____

_____

_____

_____

_____

_____

_____

_____

_____

SPREAD THE LIGHT

51

*"But when the Helper comes, whom I shall send to you from the Father,
the Spirit of truth who proceeds from the Father, He will testify of Me."*
JOHN 15:26

*O*ur failure now is that preachers ignore the Cross and veil Christ with sapless sermons and superfine language. They don't just present Him to the people plainly, and that is why I believe that the Spirit of God doesn't work with power in our churches. What we need is to preach Christ and present Him to a perishing world. The world can get on very well without you and me, but the world cannot get on without Christ, and therefore we must testify of Him; and the world, I believe, today is just hungering and thirsting for this divine, satisfying portion. Thousands and thousands are sitting in darkness, knowing not of this great light, but when we begin to preach Christ honestly, faithfully, sincerely, and truthfully—holding Him up and not ourselves, presenting Christ and not our opinions—then the Holy Spirit will come and bear witness. He will testify that what we say is true.

The Spirit's presence is one of the strongest proofs that our Gospel is divine, that it is of divine origin. Remember, when Christ was preparing to leave the world He said, "He shall glorify me," and "He will testify of me." And so the Spirit is here now, as in the days of Pentecost, when Christ was preached clearly. The message Peter preached should be the same: "Therefore let all the house of Israel know assuredly that God has made this Jesus, whom you crucified, both Lord and Christ" (Acts 2:36). When Peter said this, the Holy Spirit descended upon the people and testified of Christ—bore witness in signal demonstration that all this was true.

RESPONDING IN PRAYER

*"Lord, today more than ever the Cross is a stumbling block and
offensive to the world. Help me to make it attractive by how
I present it and how I live but never compromise its demands."*

Continuing in prayer . . .

_____

_____

_____

_____

How is the Cross always going to be at odds with the world no matter how much self-sacrifice and service accompanies it? How do you remain true to the message even if it is unpopular?

_____

_____

_____

_____

_____

_____

_____

_____

_____

_____

SPIRITUAL GOALS FOR THE WEEK

_____

_____

_____

_____

_____

_____

_____

DUST TO DUST

52

O death, where is thy sting? O grave, where is thy victory?
1 CORINTHIANS 15:55 KJV

I well remember how I used to look on death as a terrible monster; how he used to throw his dark shadow across my path; how I trembled as I thought of the terrible hour when he should come for me; how I thought I should like to die of some lingering disease such as consumption, so that I might know when he was coming.

It was the custom in our village to toll from the old church bell the age of anyone who died. Death never entered that village and tore away one of the inhabitants but I counted the tolling of the bell. Sometimes it was seventy, sometimes eighty; sometimes it would be down among the teens, sometimes it would toll out the death of someone of my own age. It made a solemn impression upon me. I felt a coward then. I thought of the cold hand of death feeling for the cords of life. I thought of being launched forth to spend my eternity in an unknown land.

As I looked into the grave and saw the sexton throw the earth on the coffin lid, "Earth to earth—ashes to ashes—dust to dust," it seemed like the death knell to my soul.

But that is all changed now. The grave has lost its terror. As I go on toward heaven I can shout—"O death, where is thy sting?" and I hear the answer rolling down from Calvary—"buried in the bosom of the Son of God." He took the sting right out of death for me and received it into His own bosom. Take a hornet and pluck the stinger out; you are not afraid of it after that any more than of a fly. So death has lost its sting. That last enemy has been overcome, and I can look on death as a crushed victim.

RESPONDING IN PRAYER

"Lord, I am reminded of death daily because it is part of our fallen world. At the same time, I need Your perspective to see death defeated and redeemed by Your life at every turn."

Continuing in prayer . . .

How have the deaths of other believers that you have experienced affected you?
Have they brought sadness and fear or joy and hope?

_____

_____

_____

_____

_____

_____

_____

_____

_____

SPIRITUAL GOALS FOR THE WEEK

_____

_____

_____

_____

_____

_____

_____

_____

_____

JAMES S. BELL, JR. serves as acquisitions manager at Moody Press and has received cover credit for more than fifteen books that he compiled, edited, or introduced. His specialty is classic literature, inclusing revisions of *Quo Vadis* and *Ben Hur.* He lives in West Chicago with his wife, Margaret, and children: Rosheen, Brendan, Brigit, and Caitlin.

Moody Press, a ministry of Moody Bible Institute,
is designed for education, evangelization, and edification.
If we may assist you in knowing more about Christ
and the Christian life, please write us without obligation:
Moody Press, c/o MLM, Chicago, Illinois 60610.